STBAC

1

Educating Older People: Another View of Mainstreaming

June Sark Heinrich

PHI DELTA KAPPA
EDUCATIONAL FOUNDATION

JUNE SARK HEINRICH

June Sark Heinrich is an instructor in rhetoric and composition at Triton College, River Grove, Illinois. She received the B.A. and M.A. degrees from the University of Chicago and M.Ed. and Ph.D. degrees from Loyola University of Chicago. Her area of specialization is philosophical/historical foundations of education. She is also a reading and writing specialist. She is a member of the Loyola University Chapter of Phi Delta Kappa.

She has been a teacher and administrator at several levels of schooling. She helped organize and was the first teacher-director of the Oak Community School and Workshop for the developmentally disabled in Oak Park, Illinois. She directed a church school at the Third Unitarian Church of Chicago and managed an Indian school sponsored by the Native American Committee in Chicago.

She has held many positions in educational publishing, including managing editor of the professional journal *Educational Screen and Audiovisual Guide* and director of new product development for Instructional Dynamics, Inc. in Chicago. She has written and edited many teaching materials, especially in the area of reading. Most recently, she edited a series of books for the Scott, Foresman Adult Reading program.

Series Editor, Derek L. Burleson

Education for Older People: Another View of Mainstreaming

By June Sark Heinrich

Library of Congress Catalog Card Number 82-060801
ISBN 0-87367-181-3

Bloomington, Indiana

This fastback is sponsored by the University of Southern California Chapter of Phi Delta Kappa, which made a generous contribution toward publication costs.

Table of Contents

Introduction

What is the worst discrimination in America? Against blacks? Against Hispanics? Against women? Against gays? No way. The worst discrimination in America is against old people.

—*Andrew M. Greeley*[1]

The stereotype of old age as a time of passivity, incapacity, and inactivity is being challenged in the United States. Many people are discovering that living longer does not lead to loss of interest in or need for work, love, sex, civic participation, artistic expression, physical activity, and mental activity. Although many older people still live within the stereotype of old age, many others demand acceptance into the mainstream of life as persons with needs common to people of all chronological ages.

The mainstream of life includes the mainstream of education, which includes whatever is offered in elementary and secondary schools, colleges and universities, and business and industrial training schools; mainstream education means formal, credential-giving schooling as distinguished from informal or personal education. The term *mainstreaming* commonly refers to the field of special education and integrating children with handicaps into regular classes and schools rather than segregating them in special, separate classes and schools. I am making a case for mainstreaming older people into regular classes and schools rather than segregating them in special, separate groups on the basis of age. As I shall use the term *mainstream education,* it refers both to mainstreaming into regular classes and schools and into the main educational institutions of our society.

I shall use the term *older people* rather than such terms as the *aged,* the *elderly,* and *senior citizens* or *seniors* because these latter terms have negative and often patronizing connotations. At what age do people become "older people"? Society tends to view persons between ages 50 and 60 as older people, and many in this age bracket view themselves as older people as they begin to think about retirement at age 65. Today a distinction is sometimes made between the young-old—those between about 50 or 55 and 70 or 75—and the old-old—those over 70 or 75. I suspect the distinction is being made primarily by those between 50 and 70. I prefer not to make that distinction but rather shall use the term *older people* to refer to all people near, at, or beyond the midcentury point in life.

The general problem I am concerned with is ageism, which has been defined as follows:

> Ageism is any attitude, action, or institutional structure which subordinates a person or group because of age or any assignment of roles in society on the basis of age. Ageism is usually practiced against older people, but it is also practiced against younger people. Ageism can be individual, cultural, or institutional and it can be intentional or unintentional.[2]

The specific problem I wish to address in this fastback is the exclusion of older people from much of mainstream schooling, especially at elementary and secondary levels. Schooling in our society is still viewed as only or mainly for children and youth. While many people support and promote the concept of lifelong learning, they do not see much, if any, of this learning for older people as taking place in a formal educational setting along with younger people. For many adult educators, lifelong learning as it applies to older people is and should be mainly self-directed learning or learning in informal groups in churches or synagogues, senior citizens' centers, and similar organizations outside mainstream educational institutions. If included within regular school and college programs, older adults are to be offered mostly informal, noncredential types of learning experiences.

Perhaps as a consequence, much education offered older people tends to be of a passive nature, not requiring hard thought and homework—a kind of high-class entertainment suitable for passing the time until death. Although the doors of formal, credential-giving institutions are not closed to older people who are highly motivated, educators and people generally—including many older people themselves—do not see formal schooling as a right of older people; nor do they see formal education of older people as a major responsibility of schools and colleges.

A concept of formal education that excludes older people may have been justifiable in 1900 when persons over 50 or 60 represented a very small percentage of the U.S. population, but so narrow a concept of education seems both inadequate and unjust today when the number of older people is growing so rapidly. In 1900 there were only 4.9 million Americans aged 60 and older, and the average life expectancy at birth was 47. Today there are 34 million older Americans, with the average life span for men almost 70, for women 77. According to recent medical reports, the average life span in the United States may reach 85 in the not too distant future. It is estimated that every day more than 4,000 Americans reach age 65. Clearly, these statistics tell us that older people are becoming a major population group in our society. Their needs cannot be ignored, and, as the next chapter will show, not the least of their needs is education.

Educational Needs of Older People

A woman of 74 came to (Dr. Martin A.) Berezin's office recently and said, "I would like to be psychoanalyzed."

He looked at her thoughtfully, as though to ask why anyone over 70 would start psychoanalysis.

She said, in explanation to his unasked question, "Doctor, all I have left is my future."

—*Lucy Freeman*[3]

Despite the rapidly growing number of older people in our society with many years of life ahead of them, educators, the government, and people generally show relatively little concern about the education of older people, especially the *formal* education of older people at all levels—elementary, secondary, and college-university.

Elementary-Secondary Level

Most of us would agree that the major purpose of elementary and secondary schools is to give children and youth the basic skills and knowledge they need to become self-fulfilling and contributing members of society as workers, citizens, family members, and parents. While we may deplore the fact that many young people leave school without adequate skills and knowledge, it is generally accepted that the education of children and youth is the primary responsibility of the schools.

If we agree that basic skills and knowledge are necessary for young people if they are to have full lives and contribute to society, then should not a basic education also be necessary for older people? Many older people have not had the opportunity to acquire a formal education. Many immigrants have never attended schools in this country. Many people born in this country attended schools for too short a time to learn very much or attended schools that were inadequate. Whatever the reason, according to the U.S. Census Bureau 1.4 million Americans are illiterate. They cannot read or write at all. Within the last century, the illiteracy rate for the entire U.S. population has fallen from 20% to 1%, but the illiteracy rate of older people remains extremely high. It is estimated that 30% of Americans over 65, about 7 million people, are illiterate. In addition to the number of total illiterates in our society, growing numbers of people are functionally illiterate—they do not have adequate knowledge and skills to carry out the tasks of daily successful living. Estimates of the number of Americans over the age of 18 who are functionally illiterate range from 23 to 64 million.

In the early part of this century, schools served many illiterate and poorly educated adults, particularly immigrants, in our big cities. But adult classes virtually disappeared in the depression years of the 1930s. Education of adults was considered a luxury schools could not afford. Throughout the country today, elementary schools, with a few exceptions, assume no or very minor responsibility for the formal education of adults. Yet the idea that schools should serve older as well as younger people has had recent support from the highest level. During the presidency of Jimmy Carter, an administration official said, "We want to look to the schools as family-service centers, serving the elderly and adults as well as children."[4]

It might be argued that the time is not right for advocating the inclusion of adults in elementary-secondary programs because the schools already have too many problems without money or ideas to solve them. On the other hand, the time would seem to be precisely right because school enrollments are declining and many schools are being closed. If there were sufficient support for adult classes, there would be room for adults in many elementary and secondary schools.

College-University Level

Colleges in the United States are entering a period of severe financial cutbacks and competition for students. The immediate problem is money. The long-term problem is the declining birthrate of the 1960s. Birthrate statistics tell us that the supply of potential freshmen will not drop in absolute numbers until the mid-1980s. The declining enrollment of young people, however, has been balanced to some extent by the increasing enrollment of older students. One-third of all college students are now older than the traditional 18- to 22-year-olds. These older students are mainly in their late 20s and their 30s. People over 55 made up only 9.5% of older college students in 1975.

Today it is still considered newsworthy when persons over 50 or 60 pursue diplomas or degrees. For example, the *Chicago Weekly Review* (28 July 1979) reports that "Mary McGowan, 79, received her G.E.D. (high-school equivalency) certification along with 100 other adults . . . She plans to enroll in a college program." A *New York Times* (11 September 1977) article reports that Barry Gersh entered Harvard University as a freshman at the age of 63. Gersh, like many older people, found that the doors of higher education are not as open to older people as to younger people. He says that he had to "bother" the Harvard admissions office until they agreed to let him in. Frances Purcie, 52, sued the University of Utah for denying her admission, charging that openings in the graduate school were reserved for younger students. A brief cited a federal-court ruling that discrimination against older people violated the U.S. Constitution.[5] James H. Petrie, at first accepted into a Merchant Marine training program at a Texas college on the basis of test scores and general qualifications, was rejected when it was discovered that he was 71. Since he already had a bachelor's degree in aeronautical engineering, he said he could complete the Merchant Marine training in three years and go on active duty. He pointed out that many Merchant Marine officers are in their 70s. Petrie plans to sue to get back his right to the education he wants and needs and for which he is well qualified.[6]

It can no longer be argued that older people are not able to benefit from higher education. Much past research on older people was based on disabled and institutionalized older people, who make up only about 4% of those over 65. Such research has often been used to support the traditional view of older people as sickly, senile, and sexless. Today a growing body of research indicates that aging does not necessarily bring about ill health and limited intellectual ability. Furthermore, recent research suggests that most older people would stay physically and mentally healthier if they were not encouraged or forced into retirement and out of the mainstream of life.

Another argument that is sometimes used to justify exclusion of older people from formal education is that the main purpose of education is vocational preparation and youth is the proper time for such preparation. In today's society people cannot be prepared in their youth for lifetime work. The nature of work is constantly changing, and the future of many types of work is uncertain. Middle-aged and older adults need to be able to return to school for vocational training or retraining—and increasing numbers are doing just that.

Another reason sometimes given for excluding older people from formal education is that the young and the old cannot learn well together in the same classes. The growing numbers of older people in regular college classes, however, are challenging the idea that students must be segregated by age in order to learn well. Age-integrated education would seem to serve the interests of both young and old. Older people need to know what younger people are thinking. Younger people can learn from older people, who have lived through the history that younger people can only read about or see and hear in audiovisual media. Older people can bring to classrooms a wealth of experiences, high motivation, and a seriousness of purpose. Some of them may have physical disabilities and slower memories, but these disabilities can be accommodated for older people just as they are for younger handicapped students. People of all ages—as well as of both sexes and of many racial and ethnic backgrounds—need to think and talk together, not only about the past but about the future.

Perhaps the most compelling reasons for including older people within mainstream formal education are to be found in our nation's history and democratic traditions. In the next chapters I shall review the historical trend toward including all groups of people within mainstream education and discuss the democratic ideals that support universal, age-inclusive education.

The Historical Trend Toward All-inclusive Education

Knowledge of the past is the key to understanding the present.

—*John Dewey*[7]

In the course of their historical development, schools in the United States have become progressively more inclusive. Step by step, American educational institutions have opened their doors to the poor as well as the prosperous, to females as well as males, to racial and ethnic minorities as well as the white majority, and to the handicapped as well as the nonhandicapped. The trend in American education has been toward all-inclusive, universal education. Nevertheless, as pointed out earlier, generally formal education has been viewed as primarily or solely for children and youth. Attendance in school was made compulsory as a way of insuring that all children receive the education thought necessary for the public welfare in a democracy. Thus the idea of universal education for children and youth has become widely accepted.

I am arguing that the concept of universal education should be expanded to include older people of all ages. I do not mean that adults should be compelled to attend school. (Some would even argue that compulsory attendance is no longer a desirable or realistic goal for young people.) My argument is that formal education at all levels should be as available to adults, including those over 50, as it is to children and youth. At least at the college level, and perhaps also at the secondary level, younger and older students should attend the same classes; and all educational institutions, including elementary schools, should assume responsibility for the education of adults as well as children and youth. The time has come for general support of the concept of formal education as a lifelong experience, with people moving in and out of educational institutions many times in their lifetimes depending on their needs and interests.

Such age-integrated universal education is consistent with the historical development of mainstream schooling in the United States—schooling that was at first limited to white, well-to-do males and that was expanded gradually over the years to include all groups the public was finally convinced needed and justly deserved formal education: the poor, females, blacks and other ethnic groups, and the handicapped.

Traditional Reasons for Excluding Groups

It has taken a long time for all of these groups to be included within mainstream education. They were all excluded from schooling in the past for about the same reasons, and these reasons are used today, either openly or implicitly, to exclude older people. Since these reasons were ultimately rejected in the case of other groups, I maintain that these same reasons should and will be rejected in the case of older adults. What are these reasons?

They are mentally inferior. A common argument used in the past to justify the exclusion of certain groups from formal education, especially rigorous intellectual education, was that the groups were mentally inferior. Women, for example, were considered mentally inferior at many times in the past. Even that champion of democracy Thomas Jefferson held that women are unfit in brains and character for undertaking serious study.

Like women, older people have traditionally been regarded as mentally inferior. Older people have been stereotyped as persons with deteriorating mental functions—persons who no longer belong in the mainstream of school, office, and factory. Women have broken away from the stereotype of mental inferiority and are increasingly joining the mainstream of life in all areas. While a few still doubt the mental ability of women, many—including some older people themselves—still seem to doubt the learning capacity of those over 50 or 60 or 70. Yet the evidence is clear that mental deterioration is by no means inevitable as one grows older.

Like women, blacks have been stereotyped in history as mentally inferior and unsuited for higher academic learning. The traditional picture of the dull-witted black is not very different from the traditional picture of the dull-witted old man or old woman of any color.

Even in the case of people with genuinely limited mental ability, there is no justification for excluding them from education. We have now generally accepted the premise that high academic ability is not necessary in order to benefit from formal education. The mentally handicapped have won their place in mainstream education—or at least their right to such a place. Older people of all abilities can also claim their place in the mainstream.

They do not need formal education. Another historical reason for excluding certain groups from schooling was that formal education was inappropriate to their station or role in life. It has been said of the poor, females, blacks, the mentally and physically handicapped, *and older people* that they do not need much if any formal education since it is inappropriate to their time of life or role in life. Gradually all of these groups—except older people—have won their right to pursue education and jobs in the mainstream. The attitude persists, however, that since the future of older people is limited, they should not engage in formal education demanding rigor and leading to diplomas or degrees or jobs. Since one of four persons aged 65 today can expect to live into his or her 80s, it is my conviction that *all* older people should have the opportunity to pursue an education for whatever future goals they desire. Few would deny a terminally-ill young person the right and encouragement to finish work, or even start work, for a diploma or degree. Why should we deny an older person the same right and encouragement?

They should have a separate, special education. In the past, education was justified for some groups so long as it was a special kind of education in separate schools or classrooms away from the educational mainstream. Likewise, older people have been offered special, separate programs designated for "seniors." *Some* older people (as well as *some* women, racial minorities, and handicapped persons) do need to have separate and special education *some* of the time in order to gain the self-confidence and skills denied them by past discrimination. The direction for the future, however, should be toward mainstream schooling for older people in age-integrated groups. The argument that women, blacks, and handicapped people should have special, separate schooling has been demolished in the course of history. It is now time to demolish the argument that all or even most older people need special, separate education.

They are unpleasant to look at and to be with. This argument for excluding groups from mainstream education may not be openly expressed these days, but the attitude persists, particularly in the case of the handicapped. Older people are often grouped with the handicapped. Governmental regulations frequently refer to the "elderly and handicapped" as if the two groups were interchangeable. Some older people clearly are handicapped, but most are not, except in the sense that society handicaps them by its attitudes and treatment. Grouping older people and handicapped people together does an injustice to both groups, reinforcing the stereotype that older people are handicapped and suggesting that the handicapped of all ages fit the stereotype of old age.

Younger people may sometimes object to older people because of their appearance and habits. Perhaps younger people are uneasy about being reminded that they are aging and will be older people themselves some day. In a society that makes a cult of youth, it may be unsettling to look at wrinkled faces, bent backs, and arthritic hands. On the other hand, many older people do not fit the physical stereotype of old age. In any case, older people as well as handicapped people of any age cannot justly be denied the right to mainstream education because of physical appearance.

To summarize, some of the main reasons used in the past to exclude females, blacks, the handicapped, and other groups from mainstream education apply also to older people. The law of the land has granted these once-excluded groups access to mainstream education at all levels. It is now time for older people to be granted all mainstream educational opportunities at all levels. As will be shown in the next chapter, this country's ideals support mainstream education for older people.

Ideals Supporting Mainstream Education for Older People

> Two of the American ideals which go back to colonial days . . . are the concepts of individual worth and universal educational opportunity.
>
> —*Robert E. Potter*[8]

Education in the past and into the present has commonly meant education of the young. The traditional assumptions behind formal education of the young, however, point to the need today for a new view of formal education as lifelong. What are these assumptions? And how do they apply to older people?

Education as Preparation

One of the main assumptions is that education is preparation for life. The current concern about mastering basic skills reflects this view of education as providing at least minimal preparation for life. The view of education as preparation is also reflected in the advice parents and educators generally give young people: "Stay in school. It will pay off." The common view of education solely as preparation for life may be in conflict with the view that education should be lifelong if one includes formal education within the fold of lifelong education. We think of preparation in relation to a future, presumably a rather long future. Thus education as preparation would appear to be primarily for children and youth. They have a future; old people do not. Or do they?

Do 65-year-olds have a future in society? Certainly they do in the United States. Increasing numbers of them will live in good health for at least another 20 years. Many of them may need educational preparation for new jobs. Many thousands who lack functional literacy will surely need educational preparation for future living as citizens and workers. Cannot the concept of education as preparation for future life apply to older people as well as to younger people? The only argument for denying preparatory formal education to older people seems to be that their future is shorter than that of youth. They probably will have a shorter time in which to contribute to life and to enjoy life. But is a future of 20 or 30 years—or even 10 or 5 years—too short a time in which to enjoy life and to contribute to life? Would we deny education to a young person with only a few years to live? It would seem to me unjust in either case to deny education as preparation for a future, however short. But some maintain that education should not even be thought of as preparation for future life.

Education as Continuous Growth

Philosopher-educator John Dewey is perhaps the most famous American critic of the idea of education as preparation for life. In *Democracy and Education* he wrote:

> What is to be prepared for is, of course, the responsibilities and privileges of adult life. Children are not regarded as social members in full and regular standing. They are looked upon as candidates; they are placed on the waiting list. The conception is only carried a little farther when the life of adults is considered as not having meaning on its own account, but as a preparatory probation for "another life."[9]

Instead of education as preparation, Dewey viewed education as growth leading to more growth: a process, not an end. Although he saw education as much broader than schooling, he did view—and discuss—schooling as a part of the education of young people. Since there were not great numbers of those over 50 when *Democracy and Education* was published in 1916, perhaps Dewey did not feel the need to deal with the subject of schooling for older people. But in a later book, *Problems of Men,* published in 1946 and republished as *Philosophy of Education* in 1975, he wrote:

> I may say that our present system is highly defective in opportunities for directed continuation of education. It is no disparagement of present efforts in "adult education" to say that the *continued* education of those who have left school should long ago have been made a paramount interest of public education.[10]

Although it is not clear that "public education" means "public schooling," it is clear that Dewey's concept of education as continuous growth rather than as preparation for life applies to people of all chronological ages.

Education as an End

Many other educators have objected to the view of education as preparation for life, particularly vocational preparation, for a different reason: they see education as an end in itself rather than as a means to some utilitarian end such as employment. Education as an end, education as continuous growth, education as preparation—all of these views, in my opinion, justify the formal education of older people. Older people need preparatory education—for high school or college, for jobs, for citizenship, for family living, for leisure time. Older people need to continue to grow intellectually. Whether one views education as a means or as an end, it should be available to older people as well as younger people. Mainstream formal education is not only appropriate but a right according to a second major philosophical assumption underlying education in the United States: Everyone should have an equal opportunity to be educated.

Equal Opportunity

However difficult it may be to define "equal" and however impossible it may be to make educational opportunities genuinely equal, this country's historic commitment to equal educational opportunity would seem to require at least that the doors of formal education at all levels be fully open to members of all groups in our society, including the growing numbers of older people.

The federal government has formally recognized the right of older people to education in the Lifelong Learning Act of 1976, the first federal statute dealing specifically with the education of older people. It hardly seems likely that lifelong education, which remained unfunded under the administration of former President Carter, will be funded under President Reagan. For possible future implementation, however, the Lifelong Learning Act does offer a statement of federal support for the idea that "American society should have as a goal the availability of appropriate opportunities for lifelong learning for all its citizens without regard to restrictions of previous education or training, sex, age, handicapping condition, social or ethnic background, or economic circumstance."[11]

Some may argue that older people have already had their equal opportunity to education in their youth, but many older people in this country have had no formal education at all, or very little. The number of total illiterates (especially among older people) and of functional illiterates (among younger and older adults) in the United States testifies to lack of adequate educational opportunity in the past.

There is legal precedent for providing educational opportunities for adults who were denied public education as children. In the case of *Lebanks* v. *Spears*, the court dealt with the issue of whether persons harmed by a previous denial of their right to education had a right to compensatory education. The court ordered that education and training opportunities be made available to mentally retarded persons over the age of 21 who were not given such opportunities when they were children. This case suggests that successful legal action might be taken to provide education and vocational training for any adults, whatever their age, who had no education—or very little or inadequate education—as children, and who can be shown to have been harmed by the lack of equal opportunity to education.

Some might argue that equal opportunity to education means only preparatory education for future life and that older people have no need for such preparatory education. I have already answered that argument by pointing out that many older people need preparation for jobs and other life activities as much as do younger people. Furthermore, if education is viewed as an end in itself or as a process of continuing growth, there would be no justification for excluding older people of all ages from all levels of formal education, unless one denies the worth of older people or their ability to grow intellectually.

Justice and Human Dignity

Another assumption underlying American education is that everyone should be treated as a person of dignity and worth. From all points of view, it would seem a matter of simple justice to extend equal educational access to all mainstream educational institutions and services to all older people.

No theory of justice, it seems to me, can deny equal educational opportunity to older people. Those who view older people as of less value than younger people because they have fewer years left to live are either openly or implicitly basing their view on instrumental value. It is very difficult, if not impossible, to measure the instrumental value of a person of any age over any period of time. Is the contribution that a person might make to society between the ages of 65 and 75 likely to be less valuable than the contribution of a person between the ages of 20 and 30, or 30 and 40, or 40 and 50? Is a person's value to be measured by his or her contribution to the gross national product? Who can determine whether a younger person makes a greater contribution than an older person, even someone well beyond the age of 50? Are people to be valued, like things, by their utility? Are people to be regarded as means to ends?

According to philosopher Immanuel Kant, "We value other people *because* they are other. The proper, sane, and rational way to view them . . . is as ends in themselves, not as means to any ends of ours, however exalted."[12] Kant saw people—people of all chronological ages—as having, not usefulness, but something very different: dignity. Many other philosophers as well as many political and religious leaders have proclaimed the dignity of all human beings. The United Nations Universal Declaration of Human Rights and ensuing covenants on human rights recognize the dignity and basic rights of all people, including the right to education "directed to the full development of the human personality and the sense of its dignity."[13]

If it is argued that it is not an affront to older persons' dignity to deny them instrumental education, such as job training, I would point out that in our society a job, or at least an opportunity for employment, is essential to the dignity of adults of any chronological age. I would also point out that in our educational system, it is very difficult to separate education that prepares for jobs from nonvocational, liberal education.

If American democractic ideals as well as American history support equal educational opportunity for older persons, is there any evidence that formal education in the United States is changing to accommodate those over 50? The answer is "yes, but . . . ," as we shall see in the next chapter.

Some Promising Trends

> The community college is an especially good place for mixing the generations. It provides an opportunity for the retired army officer who never studied Plato to sit next to the 17-year-old girl who never heard of Plato. It is one of the very good ways for people of all ages to relate to each other.
>
> —*Margaret Mead*[14]

In higher education, the trend toward acceptance of older people within mainstream education is clear. The college crowd is rapidly graying. Spurred by declining youth enrollments and a growing older population, many colleges and universities are offering older students a wide variety of enticing educational opportunities: credit and non-credit courses given both on the main campus and in local communities; four-year college programs that offer credit for life experience; courses offered on weekends and during summers; correspondence, radio, and TV courses; and external degree, part-time programs. Some specific examples of programs that reach out to older people are described below.

Programs and Students

The University Without Walls, headquartered in Yellow Springs, Ohio, is composed of 31 colleges and universities throughout the United States. Each of its programs leads to a bachelor's degree and is individually designed by the student with faculty assistance.

A "Pioneers" project at New England College deliberately mixes students aged 55 and over with younger students, not only in lecture halls but also in dormitories, dining halls, and extracurricular activities. One of its purposes is to show the positive outcomes of intergenerational learning.

Many institutions offer weekend college-degree programs such as the Weekend College of Loyola University of Chicago, where students can take credit courses on Saturday and Sunday.

To avoid the cost and inconvenience of travel, especially for some older students, many colleges offer credit as well as noncredit courses in local communities—in schools, libraries, community centers, and similar places. "Learn & Shop," an innovative program at Indiana University-Purdue University in Indianapolis, offers college-credit classes in department stores in shopping malls.

Most of the adults who attend classes in the programs just described are under 40, but the number of those over 40 or 50 is increasing steadily. Who are the over-50 students who attend college-credit classes and earn degrees?

Joseph Williams, 72, recently earned a degree in social science from Roosevelt University in Chicago and hopes to work in the social science field. In 1977, when he began his studies, he was a retired postal clerk.

At the age of 63, Barry Gersh entered Harvard University as a freshman. Here is what he said of his choice of Harvard:

> I did not want a school that offered the educational equivalent of baby food—mashed, strained, predigested courses specially designed for the "mature" students. And I was not interested in a new career, a continuing career, or an augmented career. I wanted to be taught, marked, judged by the same standards applicable to all new college students. I wanted to be bound by the same course requirements and discipline. I chose Harvard.[15]

What did Gersh expect to find at Harvard? Although he encountered problems as a new student, he waxed eloquent about the rewards:

> But, oh, the rewards. Nothing ahead of me except the great intellects to listen to, great books to read, sharp minds to discuss with. So many things I knew vaguely or understood "generally" came into sharp focus. Light filters into great black holes of ignorance. Words, names, concepts take on describable bodies. All while engaged in the one enterprise that offers deep and abiding pleasure and has no age barrier.[16]

Edna McGhee was 65 when she went back to college. She had been working as a secretary and raising a family. She plans to major in history or the humanities. She says, "There is so much to know and so little time left . . . I'm not doing this for a job after graduation."[17]

Some older students, however, *are* training for future jobs. At Triton College in River Grove, Illinois, where trade courses include welding, automobile and diesel truck repair, and shoe repair, it is reported that more than 16% of the students are 41 and older, and some are over 80.

How do older students fare in college? Although many come with fears about inadequacy and failure, they are often characterized by their instructors as being excellent students—serious, attentive, thoughtful. Some have visual or other physical problems to deal with, but these problems do not keep them from learning. Some of them may take longer than their younger classmates to recall facts. Older people are not all the same, however, and should not be treated and taught as a stereotyped group. Some have keen eyes and ears and sharp memories. Some are seriously handicapped physically and mentally. Some fail in college; some succeed. They are individuals and should be treated as such. Some younger students may need college-preparatory classes in reading, writing, and mathematics; some older students may also need such help.

Most of the older students who are taking advantage of mainstream educational opportunities are fairly well-off, well-educated people. Postsecondary education has done far more for those on top than those on the bottom. The economically disadvantaged are thinly represented among college credit and noncredit students. Adult college students are mainly a privileged segment of society. If a person is over 50 and poor or even middle-class with little financial reserve, he or she will find it difficult, if not impossible, to secure the financial assistance given younger students to pursue higher education, especially on a part-time basis. Furthermore, admission to many graduate and professional programs continues to be difficult, almost impossible, for students over 50.

Despite inequities in the treatment of older people, colleges and universities are clearly moving in the direction of age-free education, and there is a clear trend toward age-free community education in the community college. Community colleges offer a wide variety of noncollege-level programs: literacy education; classes for those learning English as a second language; classes to prepare students for the G.E.D., the high-school equivalency test; and remedial or developmental classes in reading, writing, and mathematics to prepare students for college-level work.

No such clear trend is observable, however, in elementary and secondary schools. With few exceptions, they continue to be institutions for children and youth. Some elementary and secondary schools offer evening classes for adults, often in cooperation with community colleges or other organizations. Occasionally a school opens its daytime classes to adults. For example, in Harbor Springs, Michigan, a senior citizens' center is located in the high school with total integration of the older people into the regular school classes and activities. But most school buildings, which represent one of the country's greatest investments in real estate and facilities, are used only a few hours each day, almost never on a year-round basis and almost never on weekends.

Since it is unlikely that formal education of older adults will be given high priority in this country at present, what can be done *now* to move toward a future of age-free education at all levels of formal schooling?

What Can Be Done Now?

In higher education, some steps toward age-free education might be taken immediately. For example, colleges and universities that do not include "age" in their nondiscriminatory statements might start doing so, even though they are not legally required to do so. Triton College's statement might serve as a model:

> It is the policy of Triton College not to discriminate on the basis of race, color, creed, national origin, handicap, age, sex, or marital status in admission to and participation in its educational programs, employment policies, or College activities.

Such a statement makes clear an institution's intent not to discriminate on the basis of age. Where it is found to exist, age discrimination could be eliminated from college and university employment policies, student admission policies, scholarship and fellowship opportunities, and student activities. Thus adults of all ages could be brought into the mainstream of higher education, and colleges and universities could truly become institutions of lifelong learning.

It has been said that "the creation of a system of lifelong learning is at least as much a problem of philosophy and direction as it is of financing."[18] Educators, therefore, can do much to encourage understanding and support of lifelong learning. At elementary and secondary levels, teachers and administrators should instill in students the idea that education is a lifelong endeavor that is never completed. Furthermore, parents and other adults should be encouraged to attend school during the day and evening to learn the basic skills and subjects children are learning. Adults need to be involved in school not only to advance their children's learning but to advance their own. One of the best motivators for a young student is a parent who is also a student. Finally, educators at all levels and in all kinds of educational institutions should dispel the notion that older people are "senior citizens" who need special treatment, special segregated learning centers, and special segregated living communities away from the mainstream of life.

It will be difficult to change the stereotype of old age. Many older people themselves seem to have accepted the stereotype and have withdrawn from mainstream life, allowing their mental, physical, and creative capacities to wither from lack of use. The fact that the older population has become a lucrative market for an assortment of books, magazines, TV programs, services, and products has not helped much to change the stereotype, in my opinion, and perhaps has reinforced it.

Removal of discrimination based on age in education and employment is actually in the interest of younger people, who must bear a growing financial burden if older people—both the poor and the well-off—continue to be maintained as a nonlearning, nonworking group. Admittedly, extension of the retirement age creates other problems, such as delayed promotions or even lack of jobs for some younger people and intergenerational conflicts over educational opportunities, jobs, and use of taxes for services. These problems can be resolved, however, if people of all ages can see the need for and justice of accepting older people as full participants in education, work, and life generally.

Special benefits and services should be based not on age but on need arising from poverty, illness, handicap, or past discrimination practices. Age, like skin color or sex, should not in itself be a factor that justifies discrimination or requires special benefits or services.

Some who agree that older people can and should stay actively involved in mainstream life may argue that to live fully one need not pursue formal studies. Older people can and do take advantage of such informal learning opportunities as reading, educational TV, lectures, museums, and various kinds of community programs. Others point out that formal education is not the only or even the primary need of older people—or younger people. Food, housing, medical care, and, most of all, love are needed by everyone of every age. I would add work and the arts to that list of minimum requirements for the full life.

Although I certainly agree that formal education is not the only or the most basic need of older people, formal education *is* a main road to jobs, acceptance, and respect—both self-respect and the respect of others. Furthermore, I maintain that formal education offers challenging opportunities for intellectual growth that are as necessary at age 90 as at age 9. "Old age can be a splendid time as long as one still lives in the world of the mind," says nonagenarian Carobeth Laird. "Oh, it's grand if you can jog when you're 90, but it's more important to be able to think."[19]

What might education be like if older people joined the mainstream in substantial numbers and at all levels? The next chapter presents a view of a possible educational future.

A View of the Future

Zelda Stanke, a 70-year-old student at the University of Wisconsin at Whitewater, thinks it is good to have the elderly on campus, and she knows that her mother approves. Her mother is a student at the same school.

—*Gene I. Maeroff*[20]

In an age-inclusive system of education, schooling would no longer be viewed as preparation of youth but rather as a lifelong process, with persons expected and encouraged to make entrances into and exits out of schooling many times during their lifetimes. The traditional view of human development as a curve beginning at birth, sloping up through childhood to a peak at maturity, and then sloping down through old age would change. The new view of human development would be symbolized by a steady incline, starting at birth and moving upward through childhood and all of adulthood, perhaps right up to death.

Same Schools, Same Classes

In the new system of age-free education, there would be no separation between adult education and regular mainstream education. Some special places, such as senior citizens' centers and nursery schools for the very young, would continue to exist for those who clearly need separate learning places. Similarly, special classes and schools for the handicapped would continue to exist for those students who have a clear need for segregated learning. In general, however, the future system of education would follow current requirements regarding the handicapped—to educate everyone in the least restrictive environment, that is, in the same educational institutions and classes unless there are clearly justifiable reasons for separate, segregated education. Thus older and younger students would be mainstreamed into the same educational institutions and at least at the secondary and college levels into the same classes.

Equal Opportunity to Higher Education

In this educational future, all higher-education programs at undergraduate and graduate levels would be open to older as well as younger people. Although age might influence a decision to admit or not admit a student to a particular program, no student would be admitted to or excluded from any program on the basis of age alone. Students would be judged as individuals rather than as members of any group. Affirmative-action policies would have to continue as long as needed to bring about general equality. Special preparatory or remedial classes would be offered to students on the basis of their needs. Many of the students in these special classes would be members of groups stereotyped and discriminated against in the past in ways that reduced their self-confidence and denied them a good basic education. One of these groups would be those over 50.

Adults in Elementary and High Schools

At the elementary level, many schools would become community centers, with children and adults coming to school at the same time in the morning to get a basic elementary education. Some adults might come in the afternoon or in the evening after work. Children would do their homework in school in the evening while their parents were attending class. The community school would be something like a public library, with people of all ages using the resources available. One positive outcome of such intergenerational education might be that the discipline problems of the present-day schools would disappear or at least diminish greatly.

At the secondary level, students of various ages would attend both day and evening classes. Some older students would enroll in regular daytime high-school classes for credit. Other older students would attend evening classes along with younger students who had dropped out of school at some earlier point in their lives to go to work or for some other reason.

New Teacher Attitudes and Methods

Faced with teaching people of many different ages, teachers would develop new attitudes and new methods. The patronizing, condescending attitude of some teachers toward children and young people would disappear. Even at elementary levels, teaching and learning would be more like teaching and learning in a good graduate-level class of today. All learners would be treated with respect, assignments would be highly individualized, student discussion would be accorded as much time as teacher talk, and high expectations and their consequent results would be the order of the day.

Educare—No Special Benefits

In the educational future, government-financed "Educare" programs would assure each American perhaps 16 years of formal education, to be acquired at various times throughout a lifetime. As older people took advantage of educational opportunities and moved into the mainstream of education and life, they would increasingly see themselves as fully participating, responsible members of society. Until serious disability or death occurred, they would continue to work and to learn and to enjoy. They would not seek special benefits or services based solely on chronological age. Rather, they would demand and expect the same benefits, opportunities, and responsibilities offered younger people. Because of discrimination in the past, there would be a need for affirmative-action policies to compensate to some degree for previous injustices.

It will not be easy to make this educational future a reality. It is possible that in the future people will not go to school at all but instead will learn at computer terminals in their homes. I hope, however, that there are many younger and older people in the United States who value and will actively support demanding, disciplined, sustained, mind-stretching, goal-directed formal education centered in schools. I hope that their efforts and mine will direct formal education toward equal opportunity and just treatment for lifelong learners of every chronological age.

Footnotes

1. Andrew M. Greeley, "Ripping Off the Elderly," *Chicago Sun-Times,* 16 January 1979, p. 30.
2. "Aging in the U.S.: Facts and Figures," *Interracial Books for Children Bulletin* 7, no. 6 (1976): 11.
3. Lucy Freeman, *The Sorrow and the Fury: Overcoming Hurt and Loss from Childhood to Old Age* (Englewood Cliffs, N.J.: Prentice-Hall, 1978), p. 116.
4. "The Ace Up Carter's Sleeve," *Chicago Daily News,* 14-15 January 1978, p. 6.
5. Gene I. Maeroff, "Rising Median Age Is Affecting Education at All Levels," *New York Times,* 8 January 1978, education sec., p. 10.
6. "Eager Student Rebuffed by an Age-old Problem," *Chicago Sun-Times,* 10 September 1981, p. 50.
7. John Dewey, *Democracy and Education* (New York: The Free Press, 1966), p. 214.
8. Robert E. Potter, *The Stream of American Education* (New York: Van Nostrand Reinhold Company, 1967), p. 5.
9. Dewey, *Democracy and Education,* p. 54.
10. John Dewey, *Philosophy of Education* (Totowa, N.J.: Littlefield, Adams and Company, 1975), p. 91.
11. Richard E. Peterson and Associates, *Lifelong Learning in America* (San Francisco: Jossey-Bass Publishers, 1979), p. 298.
12. Mary Midgley, *Beast and Man, The Roots of Human Nature* (Ithaca, N.Y.: Cornell University Press, 1978), p. 354.
13. Vernon Van Dyke, *Human Rights, the United States, and World Community* (London: Oxford University Press, 1970), p. 65.
14. Maeroff, "Rising Median Age."
15. "A Freshman with Seniority," *New York Times,* 11 September 1977, education sec., p. 1.
16. *Ibid.,* p. 6.
17. School Guide, *Chicago Sun-Times,* 3 January 1982, p. 3.
18. Wilbur Cross and Carol Florio, *You Are Never Too Old to Learn* (New York: McGraw-Hill Book Company, 1978), p. 98.
19. Rita Rooney, "Carobeth Laird: An Old Woman Dreams—and Writes Books," *Parade Magazine,* 30 July 1978, p. 6.
20. Maeroff, "Rising Median Age."

Selected References

Axford, Roger W. *Adult Education: The Open Door.* Scranton, Pa.: International Textbook Company, 1969.

Blau, Zena Smith. *Old Age in a Changing Society.* New York: New Viewpoints, 1973.

Christoffel, Pamela, ed. *Senior Learning Times* (newspaper). Long Beach, Calif.: American Association of Retired Persons, National Retired Teachers Association, and the College Board, 1981.

Chudwin, Caryl, and Durrant, Rita. *College After 30, A Handbook for Adult Students.* Chicago: Contemporary Books, 1981.

Comfort, Alex. *A Good Age.* New York: Crown, 1976.

Cross, Wilbur, and Florio, Carol. *You Are Never Too Old to Learn.* New York: McGraw-Hill, 1978.

DeBeauvoir, Simone. *The Coming of Age.* New York: G. P. Putnam's Sons, 1972.

Elias, John L., and Merriam, Sharan. *Philosophical Foundations of Adult Education.* Huntington, N.Y.: R. E. Krieger Publishing Company, 1980.

Harrington, Fred Harvey. *The Future of Adult Education.* San Francisco: Jossey-Bass, 1977.

Hesburgh, Theodore M.; Miller, Paul A.; and Wharton, Clifton R., Jr. *Patterns of Lifelong Learning.* San Francisco: Jossey-Bass, 1973.

Knowles, Malcolm S. *The Modern Practice of Adult Education.* New York: Association Press, 1974.

Overly, Norman V.; McQuigg, R. Bruce; Silvernail, David L.; and Coppedge, Floyd L. *A Model for Lifelong Learning.* Bloomington, Ind.: Phi Delta Kappa, 1980.

Peterson, Richard E., and Associates. *Lifelong Learning in America.* San Francisco: Jossey-Bass, 1979.

Tenenbaum, Frances. *Over 55 Is Not Illegal.* Boston: Houghton Mifflin, 1979.

Weinstock, Ruth. *The Graying of the Campus.* New York: Educational Facilities Laboratories, 1978.

Fastback Titles

(Continued from back cover)

85. Getting It All Together: Confluent Education
86. Silent Language in the Classroom
87. Multiethnic Education: Practices and Promises
88. How a School Board Operates
89. What Can We Learn from the Schools of China?
90. Education in South Africa
91. What I've Learned About Values Education
92. The Abuses of Standardized Testing
93. The Uses of Standardized Testing
94. What the People Think About Their Schools: Gallup's Findings
95. Defining the Basics of American Education
96. Some Practical Laws of Learning
97. Reading 1967-1977: A Decade of Change and Promise
98. The Future of Teacher Power in America
99. Collective Bargaining in the Public Schools
100. How To Individualize Learning
101. Winchester: A Community School for the Urbanvantaged
102. Affective Education in Philadelphia
103. Teaching with Film
104. Career Education: An Open Door Policy

This fastback and others in the series are made available at low cost through the contributions of the Phi Delta Kappa Educational Foundation, established in 1966 with a bequest by George H. Reavis. The foundation exists to promote a better understanding of the nature of the educative process and the relation of education to human welfare. It operates by subsidizing authors to write fastbacks and monographs in nontechnical language so that beginning teachers and the general public may gain a better understanding of educational problems. Contributions to the endowment should be addressed to the Educational Foundation, Phi Delta Kappa, Eighth and Union, Box 789, Bloomington, Indiana 47401.

PDK Fastback Titles Now Available

1. Schools Without Property Taxes: Hope or Illusion?
2. The Best Kept Secret of the Past 5,000 Years: Women Are Ready for Leadership in Education
3. Open Education: Promise and Problems
4. Performance Contracting: Who Profits Most?
5. Too Many Teachers: Fact or Fiction?
6. How Schools Can Apply Systems Analysis
7. Busing: A Moral Issue
8. Discipline or Disaster?
9. Learning Systems for the Future
10. Who Should Go to College?
11. Alternative Schools in Action
12. What Do Students Really Want?
13. What Should the Schools Teach?
14. How To Achieve Accountability in the Public Schools
15. Needed: A New Kind of Teacher
16. Information Sources and Services in Education
17. Systematic Thinking About Education
18. Selecting Children's Reading
19. Sex Differences in Learning To Read
20. Is Creativity Teachable?
21. Teachers and Politics
22. The Middle School: Whence? What? Whither?
23. Publish: Don't Perish
24. Education for a New Society
25. The Crisis in Education is Outside the Classroom
26. The Teacher and the Drug Scene
27. The Liveliest Seminar in Town
28. Education for a Global Society
29. Can Intelligence Be Taught?
30. How To Recognize a Good School
31. In Between: The Adolescent's Struggle for Independence
32. Effective Teaching in the Desegregated School
33. The Art of Followership (What Happened to the Indians?)
34. Leaders Live with Crises
35. Marshalling Community Leadership to Support the Public Schools
36. Preparing Educational Leaders: New Challenges and New Perspectives
37. General Education: The Search for a Rationale
38. The Humane Leader
39. Parliamentary Procedure: Tool of Leadership
40. Aphorisms on Education
41. Metrication, American Style
42. Optional Alternative Public Schools
43. Motivation and Learning in School
44. Informal Learning
45. Learning Without a Teacher
46. Violence in the Schools: Causes and Remedies
47. The School's Responsibility for Sex Education
48. Three Views of Competency-Bas Education: I Theory
49. Three Views of Competency-Bas Education: II University of Hous
50. Three Views of Competency-Bas Education: III University of Neb
51. A University for the World: The Nations Plan
52. Oikos, the Environment and Edu
53. Transpersonal Psychology in Ed
54. Simulation Games for the Class
55. School Volunteers: Who Needs T
56. Equity in School Financing: Full
57. Equity in School Financing: Dist Equalizing
58. The Computer in the School
59. The Legal Rights of Students
60. The Word Game: Improving Com
61. Planning the Rest of Your Life
62. The People and Their Schools: C Participation
63. The Battle of the Books: Kanawh
64. The Community as Textbook
65. Students Teach Students
66. The Pros and Cons of Ability Gr
67. A Conservative Alternative Scho A+ School in Cupertino
68. How Much Are Our Young People Story of the National Assessmen
69. Diversity in Higher Education: R the Colleges
70. Dramatics in the Classroom: Ma Come Alive
71. Teacher Centers and Inservice E
72. Alternatives to Growth: Educatio Stable Society
73. Thomas Jefferson and the Educa New Nation
74. Three Early Champions of Educa Franklin, Benjamin Rush, and N
75. A History of Compulsory Educat
76. The American Teacher: 1776-197
77. The Urban School Superintenden and a Half of Change
78. Private Schools: From the Purit Present
79. The People and Their Schools
80. Schools of the Past: A Treasury
81. Sexism: New Issue in American
82. Computers in the Curriculum
83. The Legal Rights of Teachers
84. Learning in Two Languages

84S. Learning in Two Languages (Sp

(Continued on inside back c

See inside back cover for prices.